MARCO POLO

THE KID WHO TRAVELED THE WORLD

VIRGINIA GRANT

BOOKSTEM

Copyright © 2025 by Virginia Grant

All rights reserved.

No part of this book may be reproduced in any form or by any electronic or mechanical means, including information storage and retrieval systems, without written permission from the author, except for the use of brief quotations in a book review.

CONTENTS

Introduction   5

1. GROWING UP IN VENICE   15
   The Polo Family's Business   18
   Young Marco's Curiosity About the World   21

2. SETTING OFF ON AN EPIC JOURNEY   25
   A Second Trip to the East—This Time with Marco!   28
   Crossing Dangerous Lands: Deserts, Mountains, and Bandits   32

3. THE SILK ROAD AND ITS WONDERS   37
   Exotic Goods and Spices: What Was Traded?   40
   The Challenges of Travel in the 13th Century   44

4. MEETING KUBLAI KHAN   49
   Marco Impresses the Great Khan   52
   Life in the Mongol Court   56

5. ADVENTURES IN CHINA   61
   Amazing Inventions: Paper Money, Fireworks, and More   64
   Marco's Role as a Messenger for the Khan   68

6. THE LONG ROAD HOME   73
   The Dangerous Journey Back to Venice   76
   Capture at Sea and Time in Prison   79

7. WRITING HIS FAMOUS BOOK	83
The Impact of His Stories on Europe	86
Did People Believe His Adventures?	89
8. MARCO POLO'S LEGACY	93
Other Travelers Inspired by Marco Polo	96
The Age of Exploration Begins	99
Conclusion: What We Can Learn from Marco Polo	103
Appendix	113

INTRODUCTION

Venice was a city like no other. It wasn't just a place of winding canals and grand buildings—it was a center of trade, where ships from faraway lands arrived, carrying silk, spices, and stories of places few Europeans had ever seen. It was here, in this bustling city, that Marco Polo was born in 1254. His family wasn't just any family; they were merchants, traders who spent their lives traveling and doing business with people from distant parts of the world.

Marco's father, Niccolò Polo, and his uncle, Maffeo, had already traveled farther than most Venetians. They had journeyed east, deep into lands most Europeans had only heard rumors about. By the time Marco was a teenager, he was eager to follow in their footsteps. He hadn't met his father until he was around 15 because Niccolò had been away for years on one of these long trading expeditions. When they finally reunited, Niccolò and Maffeo had incredible news—they were going back to the East, and this time, Marco would go with them.

Traveling back then wasn't as simple as getting on a plane or taking a train. It meant months, even years, of riding horses and camels, walking across deserts, and braving dangerous mountain paths. It was exhausting and risky. Bandits lurked along trade routes, storms could strike without warning, and illnesses were a constant threat. But for Marco, the chance to see new lands, meet new people, and experience different cultures was worth every challenge.

Their journey took them along the Silk Road, a network of trade routes that connected Europe to Asia. Along the way, Marco saw things he had never imagined—towering cities with golden rooftops, markets filled with goods he had never heard of, and people who spoke languages completely different from his own. The further east they traveled, the more Marco realized how little he had known about the world outside of Venice.

Eventually, after several years of travel, they

arrived in the court of Kublai Khan, the powerful ruler of the Mongol Empire. Unlike most European rulers, Kublai Khan controlled a vast empire that stretched across much of Asia. He was curious about the West and eager to learn more about European customs. Marco, who was now in his early twenties, quickly became one of his trusted visitors. Kublai Khan saw something in Marco—his ability to observe, learn, and communicate what he had seen.

For years, Marco stayed in the Mongol Empire, exploring cities and regions that no other European had ever described. He witnessed inventions and technologies that were centuries ahead of what was common in Europe. There were paper money, grand canals, advanced medicine, and even postal systems that could carry messages across vast distances in a matter of days. Marco paid close attention to everything, taking careful notes on what he saw.

After spending nearly two decades in the East, Marco and his family finally returned to Venice. But when he shared his stories, many people didn't believe him. They thought he was exaggerating or making things up. A world that advanced? Cities that enormous? It seemed impossible to those who had never left Europe. But Marco insisted that everything he had seen was real, and eventually, his experiences were written down in a book, *The Travels of Marco Polo*.

A Journey That Changed the World

Long before airplanes, trains, or even reliable maps, traveling across the world was dangerous, slow, and unpredictable. Few people ever left their hometowns, let alone traveled thousands of miles into unfamiliar lands. Marco Polo's journey was different. He didn't just go farther than most—he brought back knowledge that would reshape Europe's understanding of the world.

His travels along the Silk Road introduced him to new foods, strange animals, and cities filled with wonders unlike anything he had seen in Venice. He saw palaces decorated with gold, paper money being used instead of coins, and roads stretching farther than anyone in Europe had imagined possible. He learned that in some places, people drank tea every day, burned black rocks for heat instead of wood (something Europe wouldn't do for centuries), and built structures so strong and tall that they seemed impossible.

Many of the things he described were unheard of in the West. At the time, European cities were much smaller than those in Asia. Most people still used silver or gold coins for trade, while China had already developed a system of paper currency. Europeans relied on handwritten books copied one at a time, while Chinese printers used woodblocks to print entire pages much faster. Even something as simple as pasta, which is now a major part of Italian cuisine, may have been influenced by what Marco saw in the East.

His descriptions of the Mongol Empire were some of the most astonishing. In Europe, rulers controlled much smaller territories, and travel between different kingdoms could be dangerous. The Mongols, under Kublai Khan, had built an empire that stretched from China to Eastern Europe, with roads connecting everything in between. Marco saw firsthand how the Mongols maintained order, kept trade routes safe, and encouraged people from different cultures to share ideas.

Not everyone believed his stories. When he returned to Venice, people were skeptical. It wasn't just that he claimed to have traveled so far—it was that the world he described seemed too advanced. Many Europeans thought their way of life was the most developed, yet Marco spoke of cities bigger than any in Europe, bridges longer and stronger than any they had built, and a ruler who controlled more land than any king they had ever heard of.

Despite the doubts, his experiences were eventually written down, and his book became one of the most influential travel accounts in history. It wasn't just a collection of stories—it was a record of how different people lived, worked, and traded across the world. Over time, his descriptions helped other explorers, traders, and scholars realize how much there was to learn beyond Europe's borders.

Why His Story Still Matters Today

Centuries have passed since Marco Polo made his journey, yet his story continues to be studied, retold, and debated. Many explorers came after him, and the world today looks completely different from the one he traveled through. But his experiences still hold lessons that shape how people think about history, exploration, and even modern life.

One of the biggest reasons his story remains important is that it showed how connected the world already was, even in the 1200s. People often think of globalization—the idea that different countries and cultures are linked through trade, communication, and travel—as something new. But Marco

Polo's journey proved that goods, ideas, and even technologies were being shared between Europe, Asia, and the Middle East long before airplanes, the internet, or modern transportation existed. Silk and spices from China, math and science from the Islamic world, and artwork and craftsmanship from Europe were all part of a massive exchange that had been happening for centuries.

His travels also gave people in Europe a broader view of the world. Before he returned with his descriptions of China and the Mongol Empire, many Europeans had little idea of what lay beyond their own kingdoms. Their maps were incomplete, their understanding of different cultures was often based on myths, and they assumed that their way of life was the most advanced. Marco Polo's stories challenged that view. He described cities far larger than any in Europe, technology that seemed futuristic at the time, and leaders who ruled over vast territories with organization and efficiency.

The idea of exploration itself was influenced by his journey. Christopher Columbus read *The Travels of Marco Polo* and was inspired to set sail west, believing he could reach the lands Marco had written about by taking a different route. Other explorers used his descriptions to prepare for their own voyages. His book didn't just entertain people—it provided useful knowledge for those who wanted to see the world for themselves.

Trade was another area where Marco Polo's influence was felt. His descriptions of the goods available in China and other parts of Asia increased Europe's demand for silk, spices, and precious materials. The more people learned about what was available in distant lands, the more merchants wanted to find faster and safer ways to reach them. This hunger for trade routes eventually led to major developments in shipbuilding, navigation, and exploration.

The way information is shared today is also connected to what Marco Polo did. Before his journey, most people in Europe had no reliable way to learn about distant lands. His writings acted as one of the earliest forms of global reporting, giving firsthand details about places many had never heard of. Today, people can read about other cultures instantly through books, videos, and websites, but back then, having a record of an explorer's experiences was rare. His book showed the importance of writing down knowledge and passing it on, something that still matters in history, science, and education.

Skepticism surrounded his accounts, and that hasn't changed much over time. Even today, historians debate whether he truly saw everything he described or if parts of his story were exaggerated. Some believe he never actually reached China, while others argue that he must have because of the detailed information he provided. This kind of questioning isn't just about Marco Polo—it's an example of how history is studied. Just like modern historians examine evidence and sources to understand the past, Marco Polo's story reminds people to think critically about what they read and hear.

Travel has changed dramatically since his time, but his journey still serves as a reminder of the curiosity that drives exploration. Today, people continue to explore new frontiers, from the deep ocean to outer space. Just as Marco Polo's travels introduced people to unfamiliar lands, modern explorers seek to understand planets, galaxies, and the mysteries of the universe. The idea of venturing into the unknown, learning about new places, and sharing that knowledge hasn't disappeared—it has only expanded.

1

GROWING UP IN VENICE

During Marco Polo's childhood, Venice was one of the most important trading cities in the world. It sat right at the crossroads between Europe and the East, making it a perfect spot for merchants who wanted to buy and sell goods from faraway places. Ships loaded with spices, silk, jewels, and exotic goods arrived daily, bringing wealth and excitement to the city. Every street and canal was packed with traders from different countries, speaking different languages and wearing clothing that marked them as foreigners.

Markets lined the streets, packed with goods that most people in Europe had never seen before. Brightly colored fabrics from Asia, delicate glassware made by Venetian craftsmen, and rare spices from lands thousands of miles away filled the stalls. Merchants haggled over prices, arguing and bargaining to get the best deals. The air smelled of salt from the sea, mixed with the scents of cinnamon, cloves, and other spices that had traveled across entire continents to reach Venice.

The Polo family was part of this world. They were merchants, which meant they spent their lives buying and selling valuable goods. Marco's father, Niccolò, and his uncle, Maffeo, were experienced traders who had already traveled as far as China by the time Marco was born. They dealt in silk, spices, and jewels—things that European nobles and wealthy citizens were eager to get their hands on. Being a merchant wasn't just about making money; it was about understanding different cultures, knowing what was valuable, and figuring out the best way to get it from one place to another.

Trade in Venice wasn't just about goods—it was also about ideas. Because the city connected Europe with the East, it was one of the few places where people could hear firsthand accounts of distant lands. Sailors, travelers, and scholars all passed through, bringing knowledge about new inventions, unfamiliar customs, and different ways of thinking.

Some Venetians knew more about the world than kings and rulers because they had spoken to people who had actually been to places that others had only heard of in stories.

Even though Marco Polo grew up in a wealthy family, life wasn't always easy. He spent much of his early years without his father, who was away on a long trading journey. His mother likely took care of his education, making sure he learned reading, writing, and arithmetic—important skills for a merchant. But education in Venice was different from other parts of Europe. While boys in some cities studied only Latin and religious texts, young Venetians had to learn about business, trade routes, and the value of different goods.

Venice was also a city of adventure. It was built on over 100 small islands connected by bridges and canals, which meant boats were a part of everyday life. Instead of streets filled with wagons and horses, people traveled by gondolas and small wooden boats. Children learned to row at an early age, just as they learned to read and count. The sea was always nearby, reminding everyone that Venice's power came from its ability to trade and travel across the water.

By the time Marco Polo was a teenager, he had

likely heard countless stories of distant lands. He had seen merchants return from long voyages, their ships filled with goods from places most people would never visit. He had watched sailors unload crates of silk and spices from the East and listened as traders argued over prices in a mix of Italian, Greek, Arabic, and other languages. He may not have known it yet, but everything about his city was preparing him for the incredible journey he would one day take.

The Polo Family's Business

Merchants in Venice didn't sit behind counters, waiting for customers to walk through their doors. They traveled, bargained, and took risks. Trade wasn't just about selling goods; it was about knowing where to find them, how to transport them, and who would pay the best price. The Polo family understood this better than most. They weren't ordinary shopkeepers trading in cloth and pottery. They were international merchants, dealing in some of the most valuable goods of their time.

Spices were among the most prized items in Europe, and they didn't come cheap. Pepper, cloves, cinnamon, and nutmeg made food taste better, but they were also used for medicine and preserving meat. Most Europeans had no idea where these spices came from or how they were grown. They just knew they were rare, expensive, and highly sought after. The Polos made their fortune by bringing these goods from distant lands, places most Venetians could barely imagine.

Silk was another treasure. Unlike the rough wool and linen that most people wore, silk was smooth, strong, and beautiful. It came from China, but few Europeans had ever been there. Traders like the Polos didn't go directly to China; instead, they worked through a chain of middlemen along the Silk Road. A piece of silk might pass through a dozen different traders before it finally reached a noble or a wealthy merchant in Venice. Each time it changed hands, the price went up, making it one of the most valuable fabrics in the world.

Jewels and precious metals were also part of their trade. Gold and silver were always in demand, and exotic gemstones from the East were a sign of power and wealth. Some traders made their entire fortune by dealing in rare stones, buying them in one city and selling them in another for double or triple the price. The Polo family understood how to move these goods across vast distances, navigating not just land and sea, but also the complicated world of business.

Being a merchant wasn't just about knowing what to buy and sell—it was about survival. Long journeys meant facing storms, shipwrecks, and thieves. A single bad deal could cost a fortune. Merchants had to know who to trust, when to take risks, and when to walk away. The Polo family didn't just make money because they had valuable goods; they made money because they understood the business. They knew when to hold onto something and when to sell. They understood markets and how prices changed from one city to another.

Their travels took them beyond the usual trade routes. Many Venetian merchants dealt with Constantinople, Alexandria, and other important cities along the Mediterranean. But the Polos had gone much farther. They had traveled beyond the lands most traders knew, all the way to the court of Kublai Khan. By doing so, they had created business relationships that few others had. They didn't just bring back goods—they brought back knowledge. They learned new ways of doing business, new products to trade, and new connections that gave them an advantage over other merchants.

While Marco Polo was still young, his father and

uncle were already making history. Their journey to China had opened doors that no other Venetian traders had ever stepped through. By the time Marco was old enough to join them, he had already been raised in a world that revolved around trade, negotiations, and long-distance travel. The family business wasn't just about selling silk or spices—it was about understanding the world, adapting to change, and knowing how to turn opportunity into success.

Young Marco's Curiosity About the World

For someone like Marco Polo, growing up in a place like this meant being surrounded by stories. Travelers told of deserts where the sand stretched for days without end, mountains so high they touched the clouds, and cities so grand they made Venice seem small. Many people listened to these stories with amazement but never considered leaving home. Marco was different. He wanted to know more.

Most boys his age were expected to take on family trades, and for Marco, that meant business. He learned about weights, measurements, and the value of goods from different regions. He was taught how to bargain, how to recognize quality materials, and how to read and write—skills that would help him if he ever became a merchant. But numbers and business deals weren't the only things that interested him. He wanted to understand the world beyond the goods that arrived in Venice. Where did silk come from? How was it made? Who were the people growing the spices that Europeans paid so much money for?

Books weren't common, and most people relied on word-of-mouth to learn about distant places. Venice's trade connections meant that Marco had more access to knowledge than most. He listened closely whenever sailors or returning merchants spoke about their travels. He asked questions about the lands they had seen, what the people were like, what they ate, and how they lived. It wasn't just about business—he wanted to understand how the world worked.

His father and uncle had already done something extraordinary. They had traveled farther than most Venetians, reaching the Mongol Empire and meeting Kublai Khan. While they were gone, Marco had been growing up in a city that was constantly changing. By the time they returned, his curiosity had only grown stronger. He didn't just want to hear about these places—he wanted to see them for himself.

Travel was difficult and dangerous, but it was also the only way to truly understand the world. Venice had given Marco a glimpse of what was out there, but he wanted more than glimpses. He wanted to walk the streets of foreign cities, hear different languages spoken around him, and learn firsthand about the cultures that supplied the goods his family traded.

Not everyone thought this way. Many people in Venice were content with their lives and never traveled farther than the nearby towns. Some believed that places beyond Europe were wild, mysterious, and even dangerous. But Marco had heard too much to believe that the world outside of Venice was just an unknown, empty space. He had met people from faraway lands, seen goods that came from places few had visited, and heard about cities even larger than his own. If those places existed, then there was more to learn—more to see, more to experience, and more to bring back home.

His father and uncle knew the risks of travel. They had spent years on the road, navigating harsh deserts, crossing mountains, and facing dangers that most people in Venice would never encounter. Yet, they had returned with knowledge and wealth that few could match. Marco had grown up hearing about these journeys, and by the time he was old enough, he was ready to be part of one. His curiosity wasn't just a passing interest—it was the beginning of something much bigger.

2

SETTING OFF ON AN EPIC JOURNEY

For years, Niccolò and Maffeo Polo had been missing from Venice. They hadn't disappeared without reason. They had left on a journey that few would have dared to take—one that led them farther than most Europeans had ever traveled. While others in Venice traded with familiar cities around the Mediterranean, the Polo brothers had gone far beyond, reaching lands that many people back home had only heard about in rumors.

When they finally returned, their arrival wasn't just a homecoming; it was a revelation. They had been gone for nearly 15 years, and in that time, Venice had changed. But nothing in Venice could compare to what they had seen. They spoke of a ruler unlike any in Europe, a vast empire where roads stretched farther than the eye could see, and cities filled with riches beyond anything Venetians could imagine. They had stood in the court of Kublai Khan, the leader of the Mongol Empire, and had been treated as honored guests.

Their journey had not been an accident. When they first left Venice, they had only intended to travel east to trade. They made their way to Constantinople, then moved further, through lands controlled by the Mongols. At the time, Europe and the Mongol Empire were not at war, and this made it possible for merchants to travel more safely than they could through many other parts of the world. The Polo brothers followed trade routes that connected East and West, routes that had existed for centuries but that few Europeans dared to explore.

As they traveled deeper into Mongol territory, they realized they were moving through an empire that was more powerful than most Europeans understood. The Mongols controlled enormous amounts of land, stretching from the Middle East all the way to China. Trade flowed smoothly through their empire because they had built strong roads and safe routes. Unlike the divided kingdoms of

Europe, the Mongols had created a system where merchants could travel across great distances without constant fear of being robbed or attacked.

Eventually, their journey led them to the court of Kublai Khan. At the time, Kublai Khan was one of the most powerful men in the world. He ruled over China and much of Asia, commanding an empire that stretched thousands of miles. He was curious about the West, eager to learn more about the people who lived beyond his lands. When Niccolò and Maffeo arrived, they found themselves welcomed in a way they hadn't expected.

Kublai Khan was interested in European customs, religion, and technology. He asked them questions about their homeland, the way people in Venice lived, and what kind of knowledge they could bring to his empire. Before they left, he gave them an important mission—he wanted them to return to Europe and bring back scholars, priests, and experts who could teach him more about Western ways. He gave them a golden tablet, a pass that allowed them to travel safely through Mongol lands, ensuring they would not be harmed or delayed.

By the time they made it back to Venice, Marco Polo had grown up without them. He had spent most of his childhood hearing stories about his father but never really knowing him. Now, his father and uncle had returned with tales that didn't sound like anything the people of Venice had ever heard before. They described grand cities, incredible inventions, and a ruler who commanded more land than any European king. They had traveled through deserts, mountains, and lands where few Europeans had ever set foot.

A Second Trip to the East—This Time with Marco!

Leaving Venice was not an easy decision. Traveling to the East meant saying goodbye to home, family, and everything familiar. It meant stepping into the unknown, where dangers lurked along the way and there was no guarantee of returning. But for Marco Polo, there was never a question about going. The stories his father and uncle told filled his mind with possibilities, and the chance to see those places for himself was something he could not turn down.

Kublai Khan had made a request. He wanted the Polo family to return to his court, and he had sent a message asking them to bring scholars and religious leaders from the West. Niccolò and Maffeo knew they had to honor that request, and this time, they would not be leaving Marco behind. He was about seventeen years old when they prepared for the journey. By then, he had learned much about trade, maps, and the value of goods from different regions, but there was only so much that could be taught in Venice. The rest had to be learned on the road.

The journey ahead would take years. It was not as simple as getting on a ship and sailing straight to China. There was no direct route. Instead, they would have to travel across land and sea, moving through kingdoms with their own rules and dangers. They would have to cross mountains, deserts, and rivers, relying on guides and traders to help them navigate unfamiliar lands. There would be places where food and water were scarce, and others where they would need special permission just to pass through. Every step of the journey required careful planning.

Before leaving, they gathered gifts for Kublai Khan. Bringing valuable goods was not just a sign of respect—it was also a way to show that their journey had been worthwhile. Among their belongings were fine European glassware, religious relics, and letters from the Pope. These items would serve as proof that they had fulfilled the Khan's request to bring back knowledge from the West, even though they had struggled to find the scholars he had asked for.

They traveled first by sea, setting sail from Venice and making their way toward the Middle East. Their route took them through dangerous waters, where storms and pirates were a constant threat. The sea was the fastest way to travel long distances, but it was also unpredictable. If a ship was caught in a storm, it could be lost completely. If it ran out of supplies, the crew could be stranded. Every journey came with risks, but the Polo family was prepared. They had traveled these waters before, and they knew how to navigate the challenges of sea travel.

Once they reached land, they had to continue on foot and by caravan. This part of the journey was even more difficult. Ships could move quickly across open water, but crossing deserts and mountains took time. They had to travel with merchants and traders, joining caravans that moved slowly but safely through harsh environments.

The Silk Road was the path they followed, but it was not a single road. It was a vast network of trade routes stretching across Asia, connecting cities and cultures. Some parts of the route were well-maintained, with resting places and supply stations. Others were wild and unguarded, where bandits waited to attack travelers. The journey required patience and caution. They had to rely on experienced guides who knew the land, the people, and the safest ways to travel.

Along the way, Marco saw places unlike anything he had known in Venice. The architecture, clothing, food, and customs of each city were different. He listened carefully to new languages, observed how people lived, and paid attention to the way business was done. Trade was more than just buying and selling—it was about relationships, trust, and understanding how different cultures valued goods. He asked questions and took notes, eager to remember everything he learned.

The further they traveled, the more he realized how much there was to see. Some cities were wealthy beyond imagination, filled with bustling markets, towering palaces, and advanced technology. Others were small but strategically important, serving as stops for merchants crossing the vast distances between East and West. Each place had its own way of life, shaped by its geography, rulers, and history.

Traveling for years was exhausting, but it also changed the way Marco saw the world. He was no longer just a merchant's son from Venice. He was experiencing the world firsthand, learning from people who had spent their lives in lands he had only heard about in stories. By the time they neared the Mongol Empire, he had seen deserts that stretched for miles, mountains that seemed impossible to cross, and cities that thrived in the most unexpected places.

Crossing Dangerous Lands: Deserts, Mountains, and Bandits

The deserts were among the most difficult to cross. They stretched for hundreds of miles, with little more than sand, rock, and blistering heat. The travelers rode camels, which could handle the harsh environment better than horses. Camels could go for days without water and were strong enough to carry heavy loads, but even they struggled in the endless heat. The travelers had to follow specific routes, moving from one oasis to another. These were small patches of land where underground water made it possible for plants to grow, providing a rare place to rest and resupply. If they missed an oasis, they risked running out of water—a mistake that could mean death.

The wind was another challenge. It wasn't just a

soft breeze—it was powerful, whipping up sandstorms that could last for days. Sand filled the air, making it impossible to see, breathe, or move forward. Travelers had to cover their faces and wait for the storms to pass. If they strayed from the path, they could get lost, and in the desert, being lost often meant never finding the way out. Guides who knew the land were essential, leading the group along the safest routes and warning them of dangers ahead.

After the deserts came the mountains. The terrain changed from burning sand to steep, icy slopes where the cold was just as dangerous as the heat had been. The mountains were high—so high that the air was thin, making it harder to breathe. The paths were narrow, with steep drops on either side. One wrong step could mean falling hundreds of feet. Snow and ice covered the ground, making every step risky. The group had to travel slowly, often leading their animals by hand rather than riding them.

Food was a constant concern. Hunting was nearly impossible in the mountains, and there were no markets or villages to buy supplies. Everything had to be carried, and the higher they climbed, the more difficult it became. The cold made it harder to stay warm, and the wind was fierce. At night, they had to find shelter wherever they could—sometimes in caves, other times by setting up tents and hoping they wouldn't be buried by snowfall.

Then there were the bandits. The Silk Road was famous for trade, but it was also known for its dangers. Traveling merchants carried valuable goods—spices, silk, jewels, and gold. That made them targets. Bandits hid along the route, waiting for caravans to pass so they could attack. Some were small groups looking for quick riches, while others were organized gangs that controlled entire sections of the road. Travelers had to be on guard at all times.

Caravans often traveled together for safety. The more people in a group, the harder it was for bandits to attack. Armed guards were hired to protect the merchants, and everyone kept a close watch for signs of danger. If a bandit attack seemed likely, the travelers would form a defensive circle, placing their animals and supplies in the center while the guards prepared to fight. Sometimes, they could negotiate, offering a portion of their goods to be left alone. Other times, they had no choice but to defend themselves.

Despite the dangers, the journey continued. Marco Polo saw more of the world than most people in Europe ever would. He learned how traders survived in the harshest environments, how they planned their routes, and how they adapted to different challenges. Every part of the trip taught him something new—how to navigate the desert, how to survive in the mountains, and how to travel safely in lands where danger was never far away.

3

THE SILK ROAD AND ITS WONDERS

The Silk Road wasn't a single path—it was a vast network of trade routes stretching across continents. It wound through deserts, mountains, forests, and cities, connecting merchants, scholars, and travelers from Europe, the Middle East, Central Asia, India, and China. Along the way, Marco Polo saw a world that was constantly changing. Some regions were ruled by powerful kings, while others were controlled by nomads who lived in tents and moved with the seasons.

Markets were the heart of every city they passed through. These were not quiet, orderly places. They were loud, crowded, and full of movement. Merchants shouted prices, customers haggled over deals, and the air smelled of roasting meat, fresh bread, and spices from across the world. Brightly colored fabrics hung from wooden stalls, and tables overflowed with fruits and nuts that had traveled just as far as the people buying them.

Trade wasn't just about goods—it was about knowledge. The Silk Road didn't only carry silk and spices; it carried ideas. Scholars and religious leaders from different cultures met in these markets, sharing books, inventions, and beliefs. Marco Polo listened as people discussed medicine, astronomy, and mathematics, many of which were more advanced than what he had known in Europe. Some traders carried paper money, an idea that was still unfamiliar in Venice. Others spoke of technology, like printing and gunpowder, that would change the world in ways most Europeans couldn't yet understand.

The people were as varied as the goods they sold. Some wore brightly dyed robes, their fabrics woven in ways Marco had never seen before. Others dressed in heavy furs, protecting themselves from the biting cold of the northern regions. Languages blended together, creating a mix of sounds that filled the air. Marco heard Arabic, Persian, Turkic, Mongolian, and Chinese, often spoken in the same marketplace.

Food was another surprise. What people ate depended on where they lived, and Marco encountered dishes he had never heard of before. In one place, rice was the main meal. In another, noodles were served in steaming bowls of broth. Some foods were spicy, others sweet. Tea was a common drink in the East, something Marco had never seen in Venice. In some places, dairy products were a staple—fermented mare's milk was a common drink among Mongol nomads. Everywhere he went, food was more than just a meal—it was a window into the way people lived.

Religion was another difference. Europe was almost entirely Christian, but along the Silk Road, beliefs varied. Islam was widespread, and mosques with tall minarets stood in the cities Marco passed through. Buddhist temples with golden statues filled the landscapes of Central Asia and China. Hindu traditions were strong in India, and along the way, Marco also encountered people who followed Zoroastrianism, a religion that had existed for centuries. Each culture had its own way of worship, and while some rulers allowed different religions to coexist, others demanded strict adherence to one belief.

Hospitality played a large role in Silk Road

culture. Travelers were often welcomed by local families or given shelter in caravanserais—large roadside inns designed for merchants and their animals. These were safe resting places, where people from all over the world gathered for food, warmth, and conversation. Stories were exchanged over meals, and merchants shared news from distant lands.

Exotic Goods and Spices: What Was Traded?

Trade along the Silk Road was not just about moving goods from one place to another. It was about finding the most valuable items, getting them to the right buyers, and making sure they arrived safely. Every city, every marketplace, and every merchant had something different to offer. Some goods were practical—items people needed to survive. Others were luxurious, meant only for the wealthiest traders and rulers.

Silk was one of the most famous goods traded along the route, but it was not the only one. It was soft, lightweight, and incredibly strong. Unlike the rough wool and linen worn by most Europeans, silk was smooth and elegant. It was woven in bright colors, often embroidered with gold and silver thread. In China, silk production was a closely guarded secret, and for a long time, no one outside the country knew exactly how it was made. Traders who carried silk had to travel long distances, sometimes passing through multiple countries before reaching buyers who were willing to pay enormous sums for it.

Spices were just as valuable, sometimes even more. Black pepper, cinnamon, cloves, and nutmeg were among the most sought-after goods in Europe. Without refrigeration, preserving food was difficult, and spices helped keep meat from spoiling. They also made meals taste better, adding flavors that most Europeans had never experienced before. In some places, spices were worth more than gold. A small pouch of pepper could be enough to buy a house. Because spices came from faraway lands, they had to be transported carefully. They were often packed in tightly sealed containers to keep them fresh during the long journey.

Jade and precious stones were another part of the Silk Road trade. Jade was especially prized in China, where it was carved into jewelry, statues, and even small tools. It was strong, smooth, and had a beautiful green color. Traders also carried rubies, sapphires, and other rare stones from Central Asia and India. These gems made their way to European markets, where they were set into crowns, rings, and decorative objects for kings and nobles.

Metals such as gold and silver traveled both ways along the Silk Road. Some regions had an abundance of gold, while others specialized in silver. Coins were one of the most common forms of trade, but gold and silver were also melted down to make jewelry, statues, and ceremonial objects. Some merchants carried small gold bars instead of coins because they were easier to transport and could be reshaped as needed.

Glass was another prized commodity. The Venetians were famous for their glass-making skills, producing colorful beads, delicate bottles, and finely crafted windows. Their techniques were unmatched in most of the world. Glass from Venice was highly valued in the East, just as Chinese porcelain was prized in the West. Unlike the rough pottery used in Europe, porcelain was smooth, delicate, and beautifully painted. It was strong yet lightweight, making it an ideal material for dishes, vases, and decorative objects.

Tea was one of the most important goods moving east to west. In China, tea was an everyday drink, but in Europe, it was almost unknown. Traders carried dried tea leaves in large bundles, making it easier to transport across long distances. Over time, tea became one of the most important exports from China, eventually changing the way people in Europe and the Middle East drank beverages.

Perfumes and incense were highly valued, not just for their pleasant scents but for their religious and ceremonial uses. Frankincense and myrrh, two of the most famous incense resins, came from the Arabian Peninsula and were traded along the Silk Road. They were burned in temples, homes, and palaces, and were believed to have spiritual and medicinal properties. Oils and perfumes made from flowers and herbs were also popular, especially in wealthy households.

Horses were another major part of the trade network. The Mongols, who controlled much of the Silk Road, were expert horsemen, and their horses were among the fastest and strongest in the world. Arabian horses, known for their speed and endurance, were also highly prized. Traders brought horses from one region to another, selling them to armies, nobles, and merchants who needed strong animals for travel and work.

Books and knowledge traveled along the Silk Road just as often as material goods. Scholars carried scrolls and manuscripts, sharing ideas about science, mathematics, astronomy, and medicine. Arabic numerals, which are now used around the world, spread through trade routes. Paper, which was first invented in China, made its way westward, allowing books and records to be created more easily. The exchange of knowledge was just as important as the exchange of goods, shaping the way different cultures developed and advanced.

The Challenges of Travel in the 13th Century

The first challenge was the sheer distance. The Silk Road stretched for thousands of miles, connecting Europe, the Middle East, Central Asia, and China. Traveling such a distance in the 13th century meant spending months, sometimes even years, on the road. There were no trains, no cars, and no fast ways to cross the land. Caravans moved slowly, often covering only a few miles per day, depending on the terrain. Travelers had to be patient and prepared for a journey that could take much longer than expected.

Weather was another major problem. The Silk Road passed through many different climates, each bringing its own difficulties. In the deserts, the heat was relentless. The sun baked the sand during the day, making it almost impossible to walk without protection. At night, temperatures dropped drastically, and the same travelers who had been sweating under the sun found themselves shivering in the cold. Water was scarce, and if a caravan miscalculated how much they needed, it could mean disaster.

Mountains presented their own challenges. Some parts of the journey required crossing high-altitude passes where the air was thin, making it harder to breathe. The paths were narrow and dangerous, with steep drops on either side. Avalanches and rockslides were constant threats, and unexpected snowstorms could trap travelers for days. The cold was intense, and without proper clothing and supplies, people and animals could freeze.

Finding food was always a concern. There were no restaurants or stocked markets along the way. Travelers had to carry as much as they could, but supplies ran out quickly. Some areas had small villages where they could trade for more food, but in the more remote parts of the journey, there was nothing. Hunting was difficult, and sometimes the only option was to ration what little was left and keep moving. Caravans often traveled with livestock, not just as pack animals, but as a source of food in case of emergency.

Bandits were a constant danger. The Silk Road was filled with merchants carrying valuable goods—gold, silk, spices, and jewels—making them prime targets for thieves. Bandits hid in the mountains, in dense forests, or along lonely stretches of desert, waiting for the right moment to attack. Caravans had to be prepared to defend themselves, often traveling in large groups for protection. Guards were hired to fight off potential threats, and travelers always had to be on high alert, knowing that an ambush could happen at any time.

Disease was another silent threat. Long journeys meant close contact with other travelers, some of whom carried illnesses from faraway lands. There were no modern medicines or hospitals along the way. A simple infection could become deadly, and a disease that spread through a caravan could wipe out entire groups of people before they reached their destination. Some cities and trade hubs had doctors or herbalists, but getting medical help often depended on luck and the willingness of strangers.

Communication was difficult. Travelers from different regions spoke different languages, making it hard to negotiate, trade, or even ask for directions.

Some merchants learned a few key phrases in multiple languages, while others relied on translators. Still, misunderstandings were common, and a simple mistake in communication could lead to lost business, missed opportunities, or even conflict.

4

MEETING KUBLAI KHAN

After years of difficult travel, the Polo family finally reached the heart of the Mongol Empire. Their journey had taken them across deserts, mountains, and dangerous territories, but now they stood in one of the most advanced and powerful courts in the world. They were no longer just merchants from Venice—they were visitors in the palace of Kublai Khan, the ruler of China and the grandson of Genghis Khan.

Kublai Khan was unlike any leader in Europe. Most European kings ruled small kingdoms, fighting with neighboring lands and struggling to control their people. Kublai Khan, on the other hand, commanded an empire that stretched from China to Eastern Europe, covering vast amounts of land. His rule was not just about conquest—it was about organization, trade, and knowledge. He had brought together people from different cultures and backgrounds, making his court one of the most diverse places in the world.

The Mongol Empire was known for its military strength, but it was also a center of innovation. Under Kublai Khan's leadership, China had grown into a place of great wealth and learning. The roads were well-maintained, making it easier for merchants to travel. Cities were larger and more advanced than those in Europe, with grand palaces, massive markets, and systems of government that made everyday life more efficient. Kublai Khan encouraged trade, allowing goods to move freely across his empire. This was one of the reasons the Silk Road had become such a successful trade route.

Kublai Khan was interested in learning from different cultures. He invited scholars, merchants, and travelers to his court, wanting to know about their lands and customs. Unlike many rulers who saw foreigners as a threat, he valued their knowledge. He wanted to understand different technologies, religions, and ways of governing. When the Polo family arrived, they were welcomed not just as traders but as people who could bring valuable information about Europe.

Marco Polo was still young when he met Kublai Khan, but he quickly became someone the ruler trusted. He had grown up hearing about different lands, and now he was experiencing them firsthand. He paid attention to everything he saw—the way the government worked, the way people lived, and the way goods moved through the empire. Unlike most Europeans, who knew little about the East, he had the chance to see it for himself.

Kublai Khan's court was filled with people from all over the world. There were Chinese officials, Persian astronomers, Indian scholars, and European traders. It was a place where different languages were spoken and where ideas were exchanged freely. Marco Polo listened to discussions about science, medicine, and engineering—topics that were far more advanced than anything he had learned in Venice.

One of the things that impressed him most was how well-organized the empire was. The Mongols had created a system of roads and postal stations that allowed messages and goods to be transported quickly across thousands of miles. This was something that did not exist in Europe at the time. The

Mongols also used paper money, a concept that was still unfamiliar to most Europeans, who relied on gold and silver coins.

Kublai Khan ruled with both power and intelligence. He had conquered vast territories, but he also knew that keeping an empire together required more than military strength. He allowed different religions to be practiced, knowing that forcing people to change their beliefs would only cause problems. He supported the arts and encouraged the use of technology to improve farming, trade, and construction.

Marco Impresses the Great Khan

Kublai Khan was not an ordinary ruler. He was the leader of the Mongol Empire, the most powerful empire in the world at the time. He had conquered vast lands, brought many different cultures under his rule, and controlled an empire that stretched from China to Eastern Europe. He had met diplomats, scholars, warriors, and traders from every corner of the world. He was not easily impressed. Yet, when Marco Polo arrived at his court, something about him caught the Khan's attention.

Marco was still young, barely in his twenties, but

he had already traveled farther than most Europeans. Unlike many visitors who were nervous in front of powerful rulers, Marco carried himself with confidence. He had been raised in a family of merchants, and he understood how to speak to people of importance. He listened carefully, spoke clearly, and was always respectful. More importantly, he was observant. He noticed details that others might overlook, and he was quick to learn about the customs and traditions of the Mongol court.

Kublai Khan valued intelligence, and Marco showed that he was more than just a merchant's son. He asked questions about the empire, showing a genuine curiosity about how things worked. He learned the Mongolian language, which made it easier for him to communicate with the people around him. Most foreign visitors relied on translators, but Marco made an effort to understand the culture himself. This did not go unnoticed by the Khan.

One of the things that impressed Kublai Khan was Marco's ability to describe the world beyond the Mongol Empire. The Khan had heard stories about Europe, but most of the information he received was unreliable. Many travelers exaggerated their stories, making distant lands sound either more impressive or more primitive than they really were. Marco, on the other hand, spoke with accuracy. He explained how Venice operated as a center of trade, how European cities were organized, and how different rulers governed their lands. He answered the Khan's questions thoughtfully, giving him a clearer picture of the Western world.

Kublai Khan saw potential in Marco. He was young, intelligent, and eager to learn. Instead of treating him as just another visitor, the Khan welcomed him into his court. He gave Marco opportunities that few foreigners ever received. He allowed him to travel throughout the empire, visiting important cities and witnessing the way the Mongols governed their vast territories. He assigned Marco to official duties, trusting him to carry messages, deliver reports, and interact with regional leaders.

Marco did not waste these opportunities. He paid attention to everything around him. He observed the way Mongol officials collected taxes, how they maintained law and order, and how they managed trade across thousands of miles. He studied the advanced postal system that allowed messages to travel quickly across the empire. He took note of how the Mongols built roads, organized markets, and used paper money—something that was still new to Europe.

Being in Kublai Khan's court also meant meeting people from many different cultures. The Mongol Empire connected China, the Middle East, India, and parts of Europe. Merchants, scholars, and diplomats from all of these regions gathered in the Khan's palace, sharing knowledge, inventions, and ideas. Marco had the chance to learn from experts in science, medicine, astronomy, and engineering. He heard discussions about mathematics, farming techniques, and new ways of building cities. The world was changing, and Marco was in the perfect place to witness it all.

Kublai Khan's trust in Marco grew over time. He allowed him to visit distant provinces, sending him on missions that required careful observation and reporting. These journeys gave Marco the chance to see parts of the empire that few foreigners had ever seen. He traveled through regions with different climates, landscapes, and ways of life. He saw the Grand Canal, a massive waterway that connected cities in China. He visited Buddhist temples, Islamic mosques, and Confucian schools, learning about different religious traditions.

Marco's knowledge of the Mongol Empire deepened with each journey, and his ability to communicate what he learned made him invaluable to Kublai Khan. The great ruler appreciated not only Marco's ability to learn but also his ability to explain. He trusted that when Marco returned from his travels, he would give an honest and detailed account of what he had seen.

Most Europeans at the time had no idea how advanced and organized the Mongol Empire was. Marco Polo's time in the East gave him an entirely new perspective. He had grown up in Venice, a wealthy city of traders, but now he was seeing something far greater. The Mongols had built a system that allowed goods, ideas, and people to move across an enormous empire. They had established laws that kept trade routes safe and cities running smoothly. They had mastered technologies that would not reach Europe for centuries.

Life in the Mongol Court

The court of Kublai Khan was unlike anything Marco Polo had ever seen. It was a place of wealth, power, and precision, where decisions were made that shaped the future of the largest empire in the world. The Mongol court was not just one palace or one group of people—it was an entire system designed to keep an enormous empire running smoothly.

Kublai Khan ruled over a vast and diverse empire, stretching from China to parts of Europe, the Middle East, and Russia. He needed a court that could manage trade, oversee laws, and handle relationships with different cultures. His advisors were not just Mongols; they were scholars, scientists, and officials from many backgrounds. The court included Chinese administrators, Persian astronomers, Buddhist monks, Muslim traders, and Christian visitors. Each person had a role to play, and each brought knowledge from their own culture.

The Great Khan held court in the capital city of Khanbaliq, the city that would later become Beijing. It was a place of grand buildings, bustling markets, and impressive engineering. The Mongols, known for their skills as horsemen and conquerors, had also mastered administration. They had built wide roads to connect cities, established a postal system for rapid communication, and ensured that trade moved efficiently across the empire.

Life in the Mongol court was highly organized. Everything had a purpose, from the way meals were served to how messages were delivered. The Khan's palace was not just a place for luxury—it was a center of strategy and governance. Meetings were held daily, with officials bringing reports from different parts of the empire. Tax collectors, trade supervisors, military commanders, and diplomats all had responsibilities to keep the empire functioning.

One of the most surprising aspects of life in the Mongol court was the level of cultural tolerance. Unlike some European rulers who demanded that everyone follow the same religion or traditions, Kublai Khan allowed many different beliefs to exist under his rule. Buddhist, Christian, Muslim, and Confucian scholars all lived in the city, debating ideas and exchanging knowledge. This openness to learning from different cultures helped the empire thrive.

Food at the court was a reflection of the empire's vast reach. Mongols traditionally ate a diet based on meat, dairy, and grains, but in the Khan's palace, dishes from China, Persia, and India were also served. Spices from the Middle East, rice from southern China, and exotic fruits from Central Asia were common at feasts. Meals were a symbol of power, bringing together the best of the empire's resources.

Entertainment was an important part of court life. Musicians, dancers, and acrobats performed for the Khan and his guests. Mongol warriors demonstrated their archery and horseback skills in competitions. Poets and scholars recited their works, hoping to earn the Khan's favor. The court was not just a place of business—it was also a place where culture and talent were celebrated.

Marco Polo observed everything. He took note of how the court operated, how leaders made decisions, and how the empire was managed. He learned about the advanced technologies of China, including the use of paper money, intricate canal systems for transporting goods, and medical practices that were more developed than those in Europe. The Mongols had built an empire that was efficient, wealthy, and well-organized, and Marco had a front-row seat to it all.

5

ADVENTURES IN CHINA

China's cities were unlike anything Marco Polo had seen before. They were bigger, busier, and more advanced than the cities of Europe. While places like Venice and Constantinople were impressive, the cities of the Mongol Empire operated on an entirely different scale. Streets stretched for miles, markets overflowed with goods from every corner of the empire, and buildings stood taller and grander than those found in Europe.

One of the greatest cities Marco visited was Khanbaliq, the capital of Kublai Khan's empire. It was a city designed to showcase power and efficiency. The streets were wide and carefully planned, allowing merchants, officials, and travelers to move quickly through different districts. Unlike the narrow, twisting streets of European cities, Khanbaliq was laid out in a grid pattern, making navigation easier. The city had watchtowers, government buildings, and massive walls for protection. Inside, there were parks, temples, and courtyards where people gathered to discuss business and politics.

Another city that left a lasting impression was Hangzhou. It was one of the largest and most beautiful cities in the world at the time. Marco saw canals that stretched across the city, functioning like water highways. Boats carried goods and people from one district to another, making trade and travel faster than on foot. Bridges arched over the waterways, connecting different parts of the city and allowing pedestrians and carts to move freely. Markets were filled with silk, spices, and exotic goods, many of which had never been seen in Europe.

The city was also famous for its organization. Unlike European cities, where waste and pollution were common, Hangzhou had sanitation systems that kept the streets clean. Workers regularly cleared trash, and public bathhouses allowed people to stay clean, a practice that was not common in many parts of Europe. The city had hospitals, schools, and libraries, showing a level of planning and infrastructure that surprised many foreign visitors.

Paper money was widely used in these cities, something that did not yet exist in Europe. Instead of carrying heavy gold and silver coins, people used printed notes that were backed by the government. This made trade easier and allowed merchants to conduct business more efficiently. Shops accepted these notes, and banks stored wealth for traders, preventing the need to travel with large amounts of gold.

The markets were filled with a variety of foods, reflecting the diversity of China's regions. Tea was a daily drink, and entire districts were dedicated to its sale. Noodles, rice, dumplings, and roasted meats were sold in busy food stalls, giving people access to meals throughout the day. Fruits and vegetables arrived from different parts of the empire, and exotic spices flavored dishes in ways that were new to most European travelers.

Marco also noted the efficiency of the Mongol postal system. Roads connected the major cities, and relay stations were placed along the way so messengers could switch horses and continue their journey without stopping for long periods. This allowed news and goods to travel quickly, making communication across the vast empire possible.

Temples and places of learning were scattered throughout the cities, showing that religion and education were valued. Buddhism, Confucianism, and Daoism influenced the culture, and scholars debated philosophy, government, and science. Marco saw large universities where students studied subjects such as astronomy, medicine, and engineering, fields that were not as advanced in Europe at the time.

Amazing Inventions: Paper Money, Fireworks, and More

Traveling through China meant seeing things that most Europeans had never even dreamed of. It wasn't just the size of the cities or the bustling trade that made China impressive—it was the technology. The Mongol Empire didn't just rule over vast lands; it was a place of innovation, where inventions were changing the way people lived, worked, and communicated.

One of the most surprising things Marco Polo encountered was paper money. In Europe, people relied on gold and silver coins, which were heavy and difficult to carry in large amounts. Merchants traveling across long distances had to protect their money carefully, and theft was always a concern. China had solved this problem by using lightweight paper bills that could be exchanged for goods and services just like coins. The government controlled the printing of this money and backed its value, ensuring that it could be used throughout the empire.

Banks and merchants accepted the paper money, and travelers didn't need to carry bags of coins on dangerous roads. Instead, they carried government-issued notes, which could be exchanged for coins if needed. This system made trade much easier and faster. Europeans at the time had never seen anything like it, and it would take centuries before paper money became common in the West.

Another invention that amazed Marco Polo was gunpowder. Unlike anything in Europe, gunpowder was a powerful substance used to create fireworks, weapons, and explosives. The Chinese had discovered how to mix certain minerals to produce a substance that, when ignited, created a loud explosion. They used this technology in celebrations, lighting up the night sky with colorful bursts of fireworks. But gunpowder was not just for entertainment—it had also changed warfare. The Mongol army had already begun using it in battles, creating early versions of bombs, rockets, and even firearms.

Printing was another area where China was far ahead of Europe. In most of the West, books were copied by hand, a slow and expensive process that made books rare and valuable. In China, printing technology allowed books and documents to be produced much more quickly. The Chinese had developed block printing, where entire pages were carved into wooden blocks, inked, and pressed onto paper. This method allowed thousands of copies to be made in a short time, making books more available to scholars, government officials, and merchants.

Paper itself was an invention that had changed China long before it reached Europe. While Europeans relied on parchment made from animal skins, the Chinese had been making paper for centuries using plant fibers. This made writing materials cheaper and more accessible, leading to the widespread use of written records, letters, and books. Schools and government offices in China relied on paper for communication, and records were kept more efficiently than in many parts of Europe.

Compasses were another innovation that had a

major impact on trade and exploration. The Chinese had discovered that a magnetized needle would always point north, which allowed sailors and traders to navigate more accurately. While Europeans still depended on the position of the sun and stars to find their way, Chinese sailors used compasses to travel farther and with greater confidence. This invention helped merchants navigate the vast waterways of China and beyond, making trade even more efficient.

Silk production was another technological marvel. While Europeans had heard of silk, few understood how it was made. The process of raising silkworms, harvesting their cocoons, and weaving the fine threads into fabric was a carefully guarded secret in China. The finished silk was lightweight, durable, and valuable, making it one of the most sought-after goods on the Silk Road. The Chinese had developed advanced weaving techniques, creating intricate patterns and designs that were unlike anything seen in Europe.

Porcelain was another highly prized Chinese product. Unlike the rough pottery used in most of Europe, porcelain was smooth, strong, and often decorated with detailed paintings. It was made from a special type of clay and fired at extremely high temperatures, creating a material that was both beautiful and durable. Wealthy families in China used porcelain for dishes, vases, and decorative objects, and it became one of the most desired exports to the West.

Timekeeping devices were also more advanced than those in Europe. While many Europeans still relied on sundials and water clocks, China had developed mechanical clocks that used gears and weights to measure time more accurately. Some of these clocks were used in temples and government buildings to keep track of the hours, making daily life more organized.

Marco's Role as a Messenger for the Khan

Kublai Khan did not keep useless people in his court. Those who served him had to prove themselves useful, whether they were military leaders, scholars, merchants, or diplomats. Marco Polo had earned the Khan's trust by demonstrating his intelligence, curiosity, and ability to communicate well. Unlike many foreigners who visited the Mongol court, Marco paid close attention to how the empire functioned, learned the Mongolian and Chinese languages, and showed an understanding of trade and governance. Kublai Khan saw potential in him and decided to give him a role of real importance—he would serve as a messenger for the empire.

Being a messenger for the Khan was not a simple job. The Mongol Empire covered vast distances, and delivering messages across such a large territory required speed, reliability, and knowledge of the land. The Khan's messengers had to carry official letters, diplomatic orders, trade instructions, and sometimes even secret communications between different parts of the empire. These messages were often critical, affecting everything from military strategies to economic policies. A messenger who failed could cause major delays, losses, or even conflicts between regions.

The Mongols had built one of the most efficient postal systems in history. Known as the **Yam**, this system connected the empire through a network of roads, relay stations, and fresh horses. Each station had supplies and messengers ready to take over, ensuring that messages could travel thousands of miles in a short amount of time. Riders would switch horses at relay posts, allowing them to move much faster than an ordinary traveler. Some messages traveled as far as 200 miles in a single day—a speed unheard of in Europe at the time.

Marco Polo was sent on several missions across the Mongol Empire. His status as a trusted foreigner made him useful for delicate assignments, as he could report his findings without local bias. He traveled through territories governed by Mongol officials, visited provinces that were newly incorporated into the empire, and observed how different regions managed trade and law. His ability to adapt to different cultures made him an ideal messenger, as he could speak to officials, merchants, and local rulers without causing offense.

The assignments took him to places that few Europeans had ever seen. He crossed deserts, mountains, and rivers, each journey giving him a deeper understanding of the Mongol Empire's vastness. He saw cities where Persian, Indian, and Chinese merchants worked together, places where Buddhist temples stood next to Muslim mosques, and regions where different customs mixed due to the Mongol policy of religious tolerance.

Some journeys were long and difficult. The empire's roads were well-maintained, but travel was still dangerous. Harsh weather, bandits, and illness were constant threats. The Mongols had established security along their trade routes, but no traveler was completely safe. Marco Polo had to rely on the protection of the Khan's men and his own ability to navigate difficult situations. His survival depended on knowing whom to trust, how to negotiate safe passage, and how to avoid trouble in unfamiliar regions.

As a messenger, Marco also learned how the Mongol rulers governed their empire. He saw how taxes were collected, how trade was monitored, and how laws were enforced. He observed how officials handled conflicts between merchants, how they organized food and resources, and how they managed relations with other nations. These experiences gave him insight into an empire far more organized than many in Europe.

6

THE LONG ROAD HOME

Marco Polo had spent years in the service of Kublai Khan, traveling across the Mongol Empire, delivering messages, and witnessing the advanced cities and technologies of the East. He had gained the trust of one of the most powerful rulers in history and had lived in a world far beyond what most Europeans could ever imagine. Yet, after more than 20 years in China, he and his family made the decision to leave. Walking away from the court of Kublai Khan was not an easy choice, and it wasn't something they could simply decide on their own.

For a long time, Kublai Khan did not want them to go. The Polo family had become valuable to him. They understood trade, they spoke multiple languages, and they could help manage the relationships between the Mongol Empire and the lands to the west. Marco had proven himself as an effective messenger, and Kublai Khan had rewarded him with wealth and important tasks. The Khan was known for rewarding loyalty, but he also expected it in return. When people served him well, he preferred to keep them close.

Marco, his father, and his uncle knew they could not stay forever. They had left Venice as traders and had spent decades in the Mongol Empire, but their home was still in the West. They had no idea what had happened to their business, their remaining family members, or the city they had once known. They had been away for so long that Venice itself had likely changed. There was no easy way to send letters across the world, and news traveled slowly. If they wanted to know what had become of their homeland, they had to return themselves.

There was also uncertainty about the future of Kublai Khan's empire. While he remained strong, he was aging, and the Mongol Empire was not as stable as it once had been. The Khan had ruled for many years, but even the most powerful leaders could not rule forever. If he were to pass away, there was no guarantee that his successors would honor the same friendships or allow foreigners to keep the same privileges. The Mongol Empire had been built through conquest, and power often changed hands in unpredictable ways.

The opportunity to leave finally came when Kublai Khan received an unusual request. The Mongol ruler of Persia had sent a message asking for a Mongol princess to be sent to him as his wife. This was not a simple request. The journey from China to Persia was long and dangerous, requiring careful planning and protection. A group of trusted people would need to escort the princess safely across the empire, ensuring that she arrived without harm.

This mission gave Marco Polo and his family the excuse they needed. They volunteered to escort the princess on her journey, arguing that their experience in travel and diplomacy would make them useful guides. Kublai Khan agreed, but even then, their departure was not immediate. Arranging such a journey took time, and the Khan did not let them leave empty-handed. He provided them with official travel documents, supplies, and valuable gifts. He wanted to make sure they were well-prepared and that their return to the West would be a reflection of the wealth and power of his empire.

The journey back was just as challenging as the

journey to China had been. The Polo family and their group traveled by sea, a different route than they had taken when they first arrived. This new path came with its own dangers—storms, illness, and the constant threat of pirate attacks. Many members of the group did not survive. By the time they reached Persia, the Mongol ruler who had requested the princess had died, further complicating their mission.

The Dangerous Journey Back to Venice

Leaving China did not mean the journey was over. Marco Polo and his family still had to make it back to Venice, and the road home was just as difficult—if not more—than the journey that had brought them to the Mongol Empire. Travel in the 13th century was always dangerous, but after spending more than 20 years in Kublai Khan's service, the Polo family had grown used to the protection and organization of the Mongol Empire. Once they left, they would no longer have that security.

The first leg of their journey was by sea. Instead of retracing their steps overland along the Silk Road, they traveled with the Mongol princess they had been assigned to escort. The Mongol ruler of Persia had requested a royal bride from Kublai Khan's court, and a grand fleet was arranged to transport her across the ocean. This was not a small expedition. The fleet consisted of dozens of ships, carrying soldiers, noble officials, and supplies to sustain them on their long voyage.

The sea route was meant to be safer than crossing the vast Mongol lands on horseback, but it brought dangers of its own. The Polo family had spent years traveling overland, but now they faced new challenges—storms, shipwrecks, and disease. The journey through the Indian Ocean was harsh, with unpredictable winds and powerful monsoons that battered the ships. Navigating across open waters was far different from traveling along well-maintained trade roads. Ships were at the mercy of the weather, and there was little they could do if disaster struck.

Disease was another serious threat. Unlike land travel, where people could stop to rest and find fresh food, a long sea voyage meant being confined to crowded ships with limited supplies. Many of the passengers on the fleet fell sick, and once illness spread, it was nearly impossible to stop. People died by the dozens, their bodies thrown into the sea to prevent further outbreaks.

By the time the fleet reached its destination in Persia, only a handful of the original travelers remained. The Mongol princess survived, but the ruler who had requested her marriage had died before she arrived. The journey had taken so long that the political situation had already changed.

Once the Polo family completed their duties in Persia, they faced another long trip to get back to Venice. They continued overland through the Middle East, traveling through regions controlled by different rulers. Unlike their time in the Mongol Empire, where the Khan's protection had made travel relatively safe, they now had to navigate through lands where they were not always welcome. Political tensions made some areas dangerous, and they had to be careful about where they stopped and whom they trusted.

Crossing the Middle East meant traveling through deserts and harsh landscapes. Unlike the well-organized Mongol trade routes, where supplies were guaranteed at relay stations, food and water were harder to find. Caravans were their best hope for safety. Merchants and travelers grouped together, offering strength in numbers to defend against bandits. The Polo family had valuable goods from their time in China, and they had to take extra precautions to avoid being robbed.

As they neared the Mediterranean, the challenges did not end. Wars and conflicts between different rulers made it difficult to pass through some areas. Certain regions were controlled by powerful Islamic empires, while others were caught in conflicts between Christian and Muslim forces. The Polo family had to rely on their knowledge of trade, diplomacy, and language to move through these lands without attracting unwanted attention.

By the time they reached the Mediterranean coast, they had been traveling for years. The final stage of their journey was by ship, sailing across the sea to reach Venice. Unlike the massive fleet that had taken them out of China, this time they traveled on smaller merchant vessels, relying on the connections they had built through years of trade.

Capture at Sea and Time in Prison

After years of traveling through distant lands, surviving treacherous seas, and navigating foreign courts, Marco Polo finally made it back to Venice. But his return home did not bring the peaceful life he might have expected. His adventures were not over. Not long after settling back into his city, he found himself caught in the middle of a war, taken as a prisoner, and locked away in a foreign jail.

Venice was a city of traders, but it was also a city of rivals. For years, it had competed with another powerful Italian city-state, Genoa. The two cities were often in conflict, fighting for control over trade routes across the Mediterranean. By the time Marco Polo returned, tensions between Venice and Genoa had erupted into open war. The two sides clashed at sea, each trying to weaken the other's navy and take control of valuable ports.

Despite everything he had experienced in China, Marco Polo was still a Venetian merchant at heart. When the war broke out, he joined the Venetian fleet, ready to defend his homeland. He had traveled farther than most sailors, seen the organized military of the Mongols, and learned how powerful leaders maintained control. He likely believed his knowledge could be useful in battle.

The war between Venice and Genoa was fought mostly at sea, with both sides using large, heavily armed ships. Naval battles were brutal, with war galleys ramming into one another, archers firing from the decks, and soldiers boarding enemy ships to fight in hand-to-hand combat. In one of the biggest battles of the war, the **Battle of Curzola** in 1298, the Venetian fleet suffered a crushing defeat. Genoese ships overpowered the Venetians, capturing many of their men—including Marco Polo.

As a prisoner of war, Marco Polo was taken to Genoa. Captured sailors were often treated harshly, especially if they were nobles or important figures. Being a Venetian merchant with ties to powerful people did not protect him from imprisonment. He was thrown into a Genoese jail, uncertain how long he would remain there.

Prison in the 13th century was not like modern-day jails. There were no set sentences, no trials to determine a prisoner's release, and no guarantees of decent treatment. Many prisoners died from disease, hunger, or neglect before they were ever freed. Wealthy captives sometimes had a better chance of survival, as their families could pay for food, blankets, or bribes to improve their conditions. But even for someone of Marco Polo's status, there was no certainty of how or when he would be released.

While locked away, Marco found an unlikely way to turn his misfortune into something greater. He shared a prison cell with a fellow captive named **Rustichello da Pisa**, a writer from Italy. Rustichello had experience telling stories, and when Marco Polo spoke about his travels, Rustichello realized that this was a story unlike any other. He encouraged Marco to describe everything he had seen—the vast cities of China, the wealth of Kublai Khan, the inventions, the different cultures, the grand court of the Mongol Empire.

Together, they began to put Marco's journey into words. Rustichello helped shape the stories into a book, a detailed account of Marco Polo's adventures. The tales included descriptions of silk and spices, the great canals of China, the postal system of the Mongols, and the wars and customs of distant lands. No European had ever written such an extensive account of Asia before.

Marco Polo spent months in prison, dictating his experiences while Rustichello recorded them. Over time, the book became more than just a personal story—it became a guide to lands that most Europeans had never even heard of. It introduced them to new inventions, new ways of ruling, and an empire that functioned in ways they had never imagined.

7

WRITING HIS FAMOUS BOOK

Marco Polo had spent years traveling through the Mongol Empire, seeing cities larger than any in Europe, witnessing advanced inventions, and learning about cultures that were almost completely unknown in the West. When he returned to Venice, he carried something even more valuable than the riches he had brought back—knowledge. But knowledge on its own meant little unless it could be shared.

His chance to share his story came in an unexpected place: a prison cell in Genoa. After being captured in a naval battle between Venice and Genoa, Marco found himself locked away with other prisoners of war. He had no way of knowing how long he would be there, but he did have one advantage—his cellmate, Rustichello da Pisa, was a writer.

Rustichello had written adventure stories before, mainly about knights and battles, but he had never met anyone with real stories as incredible as Marco's. While the other prisoners spoke of their lives as sailors or merchants, Marco talked about his years in the East, about Kublai Khan's empire, the wonders of China, the spices of India, and the great wealth of lands beyond Europe.

Rustichello listened carefully. He was not just interested—he saw an opportunity. He knew that Marco's stories, if written down, could become something remarkable. Unlike the knights and warriors of his past books, Marco was a real person, and his experiences were not just tales but first-hand accounts of places most Europeans had never heard of.

Writing in a prison cell was not easy. Paper was scarce, and writing supplies were limited. Marco had no journals or maps to reference—everything had to come from memory. He had spent years traveling, meeting rulers, merchants, and scholars, and now he had to recall it all. He described the vast trade networks, the great cities, the customs of the people, and the things that had surprised him the most.

Rustichello turned these accounts into a written manuscript, organizing them into a flowing narrative.

The book was not just about Marco Polo's personal journey. It became a record of the world beyond Europe. It described how the Mongol Empire functioned, how its leaders governed, and how different cultures interacted. It introduced Europeans to paper money, an organized postal system, and massive cities with intricate water systems. It explained how trade routes connected distant lands and how spices, silk, and precious stones moved between nations.

The way the book was written was different from most European texts of the time. Rather than focusing on wars or religious events, it was a book about exploration, geography, and daily life in foreign lands. It painted a picture of a world that was far bigger and more advanced than many Europeans had imagined.

Once Marco was released from prison, his story did not stay locked away. The manuscript spread quickly. At the time, books were copied by hand, and different versions of *The Travels of Marco Polo* began appearing across Europe. Some versions included details Marco had not originally told. Others were written in different languages, making his stories accessible to even more people.

Readers reacted in different ways. Some were fascinated and saw the book as an invaluable record of the world. Others doubted it. The descriptions of China, India, and the Mongol Empire were so different from anything Europeans knew that some thought the stories were exaggerated or even made up. Critics dismissed Marco's accounts as fantasy, saying that the world could not possibly be as vast or as advanced as he described.

Despite the skepticism, the book became one of the most influential travel accounts in history. Over the years, it inspired explorers, traders, and even future mapmakers who wanted to understand the lands beyond Europe. It challenged old beliefs and introduced new ideas about geography, trade, and culture.

The Impact of His Stories on Europe

Marco Polo's book was unlike anything Europeans had ever read before. It told of lands that stretched far beyond what most people had ever imagined, describing vast cities, powerful rulers, and a world filled with riches and inventions that were unheard of in the West. His stories changed the way people thought about the world, influencing explorers, traders, and scholars for centuries to come.

At the time Marco's book was written, most Europeans knew little about the lands beyond the Middle East. The idea that an empire as vast and advanced as Kublai Khan's could exist seemed almost impossible. In many ways, Europe was still developing, with cities that were small compared to the ones Marco described. The roads were rough, travel was slow, and most people spent their lives in the same small villages, never seeing much beyond their local area.

The book introduced readers to new ideas about trade and travel. It described massive marketplaces where merchants sold silk, spices, and rare goods that Europeans had never even heard of. It explained how paper money worked, a concept that was unfamiliar to Europeans who were used to trading with gold and silver coins. It talked about cities with complex water systems, bridges larger than anything in Europe, and ships that were stronger and more advanced than the ones sailing in the Mediterranean.

Some people believed the stories instantly, fascinated by the idea of lands filled with wealth and new opportunities. Others were skeptical. The descriptions of China and the Mongol Empire seemed too incredible to be real. Some thought Marco was exaggerating, or even making up parts of his journey. There were no easy ways to prove whether his stories were true, so people debated them for years.

Despite the doubts, his book became one of the most copied and read texts of the time. Since printing technology had not yet been invented, books had to be written by hand, which meant that every copy of *The Travels of Marco Polo* was slightly different. Some versions were translated into different languages, while others were changed by scribes who added their own details or reworded parts of the text. No two copies were exactly the same, but the core of Marco's journey remained in every version.

Merchants paid special attention to the book. Trade had always been important in Europe, but Marco's stories showed that there were even greater markets beyond what they knew. Traders became more eager to connect with the East, hoping to find ways to bring silk, spices, and other goods back to Europe without having to rely on middlemen. The idea of direct trade with China became more appealing, even though it would take years before new routes were established.

Explorers were also influenced by Marco's writings. Even though his journey had been overland, across the Silk Road, it planted the idea that the world was much larger than Europeans had thought. More importantly, it suggested that wealth and opportunity existed far beyond Europe's borders. Centuries later, famous explorers like Christopher Columbus used Marco Polo's book as a reference when planning their own voyages. Columbus even carried a copy of the book with him when he set sail across the Atlantic.

Scholars and mapmakers used Marco's descriptions to create better maps of the world. Before his travels, European maps were often filled with empty spaces, unknown territories, and incorrect details about the lands beyond Europe. Marco's accounts helped geographers understand the geography of Asia in a way that no European had before. While some details were inaccurate or exaggerated over time, his book remained one of the best sources of knowledge about the East for many years.

Did People Believe His Adventures?

When Marco Polo's book began to spread across Europe, reactions were mixed. Some people were fascinated by his stories of the East, eager to learn about lands they had never heard of before. Others refused to believe a word of it. His descriptions of China, the Mongol Empire, and the wonders of the Silk Road seemed too incredible to be real.

One of the biggest reasons people doubted Marco's stories was that no one in Europe had ever seen a civilization as advanced as the one he described. He wrote about cities larger than any in Europe, with wide roads, organized marketplaces, and clean water systems. He explained how the Mongols had an efficient postal service, where messengers on horseback could travel hundreds of miles in just a few days. He described bridges longer and stronger than any in Venice, and ships so large that they could hold entire villages worth of people and goods. To Europeans who were used to small, crowded cities with muddy streets and unreliable roads, these claims seemed impossible.

Another point of skepticism was his mention of paper money. In Europe, gold and silver coins were the only form of currency. The idea that an entire empire could function with nothing more than printed pieces of paper seemed absurd. Readers wondered how a society could trust money that was not made of valuable metal. They had never seen a system like China's, where the government controlled the production of paper currency and ensured its value across the empire. To many, this sounded more like fantasy than reality.

His stories of exotic animals raised even more questions. He wrote about enormous serpents in India that resembled dragons, crocodiles that could swallow a man whole, and rhinoceroses that he compared to mythical unicorns. He described black-and-white bears in China that ate only bamboo—what Europeans would later come to know as pandas. Some people thought these were exaggerations, or that Marco had been tricked by the locals into believing in imaginary creatures.

Even the Mongol Empire itself was hard for some Europeans to believe. While the Mongols were feared in parts of Europe, most people knew little about them beyond the fact that they were fierce warriors. Marco Polo described them differently. He explained how Kublai Khan was not just a conqueror, but a ruler who encouraged trade, religious tolerance, and cultural exchange. He talked about Mongol laws, administration, and technology in ways that made them seem more advanced than many European kingdoms. Some readers found this hard to accept. How could a people known for war also be responsible for such a highly organized and wealthy empire?

One of the strangest doubts about his book came from the fact that he never mentioned certain things that Europeans expected to hear about. For example, Marco never wrote about the Great Wall of China, even though it existed during his time. Some took this as proof that he had never really been to China. However, others argued that the Mongols, who controlled China at the time, did not rely on the Great Wall for defense and may not have considered it important enough to mention.

Despite all the skepticism, many people did believe Marco Polo. Traders and merchants found his descriptions of silk, spices, and trade routes useful. Explorers saw his book as a guide to lands they hoped to reach. Some leaders and scholars, though unsure of every detail, recognized that his stories contained valuable information. Over time, as more travelers journeyed east, parts of Marco's book were confirmed, making even his most unbelievable claims seem more credible.

8

MARCO POLO'S LEGACY

Marco Polo may have returned to Venice, but his journey did not end when he stepped off the ship. His stories traveled far beyond his homeland, influencing explorers, traders, and scholars for centuries. The book he created in a Genoese prison did more than describe the wonders of the East—it changed how people thought about the world and inspired some of the greatest explorations in history.

At the time of Marco's return, most Europeans had little understanding of what lay beyond the lands of the Middle East. Maps were filled with blank spaces, and many people believed the world was much smaller than it actually was. Marco Polo's detailed descriptions of China, Persia, India, and other distant regions forced people to rethink what they thought they knew. His book gave a clearer picture of an interconnected world, filled with lands far richer and more advanced than many in Europe had imagined.

One of the biggest effects of Marco's travels was the way he influenced trade. His book described the incredible wealth of the Mongol Empire, where merchants had access to silk, spices, gold, and other valuable goods. European traders began looking for better ways to reach these lands. Before, most trade between Europe and Asia was controlled by middlemen in the Middle East, making goods expensive and difficult to obtain. Marco's stories made clear that if a direct route could be found, merchants could become incredibly wealthy.

Explorers paid close attention to Marco's accounts. His book described lands that seemed almost mythical to Europeans, but to explorers, they sounded like opportunities waiting to be discovered. Centuries later, Christopher Columbus used *The Travels of Marco Polo* as a reference when planning his voyage across the Atlantic. He believed that by sailing west, he might reach the lands Marco had described. Though Columbus did not find Asia, his journey led to the European discovery of the Americas.

Mapmakers also relied on Marco Polo's writings. Before his travels, many European maps were inaccurate or based on legends rather than real geography. His descriptions of cities, rivers, mountains, and trade routes gave cartographers new information to work with. Even though some details were later found to be incorrect or exaggerated, his book remained one of the best sources of knowledge about Asia for hundreds of years.

Marco's influence was not just limited to explorers and traders. His stories also helped spread knowledge about inventions and ideas that were new to Europeans. Paper money, a postal system, large-scale bridges, and advanced shipbuilding techniques were all things he wrote about that were later adopted or improved upon in Europe. While some of these technologies had already existed in China for centuries, Marco's descriptions helped introduce them to a wider audience.

Despite the impact of his book, Marco Polo's name was not always met with admiration. Many doubted his stories, believing they were too incredible to be real. Some thought he had exaggerated his experiences or included details that were not entirely accurate. Even today, historians debate how much of his book was based on firsthand experience and how much may have been added later.

Other Travelers Inspired by Marco Polo

Marco Polo's journey may have ended when he returned to Venice, but his stories traveled far beyond his own lifetime. His book, *The Travels of Marco Polo*, became one of the most influential travel accounts in history, inspiring adventurers, traders, and explorers for centuries. The descriptions of distant cities, vast empires, and advanced civilizations made people eager to see these places for themselves. While some doubted his stories, others were motivated to set out on their own journeys to confirm what Marco had written and to uncover even more of the world.

One of the most famous explorers influenced by Marco Polo was **Christopher Columbus.** Born over 150 years after Marco Polo's death, Columbus grew up in a world where *The Travels of Marco Polo* was well known among sailors and scholars. Like many others, he was fascinated by the riches of Asia and the idea that great cities lay beyond Europe, filled with gold, silk, and spices. He studied Marco's descriptions carefully, hoping to use them as a guide to reach the East. However, instead of traveling overland like Marco, Columbus wanted to find a faster route—by sea.

Columbus believed that by sailing west across the Atlantic Ocean, he could reach the same lands that Marco Polo had described. When he set off in 1492, he carried a copy of *The Travels of Marco Polo* with him, using it to compare what he encountered with what Marco had written. Though Columbus never reached China or the Mongol Empire, his voyage led to the European discovery of the Americas. Even though his journey did not unfold the way he had expected, his desire to explore had been shaped in part by Marco's writings.

Another traveler inspired by Marco Polo was **Ibn Battuta**, a Muslim scholar from Morocco. Unlike most European travelers, Ibn Battuta was already familiar with trade routes connecting Asia, the Middle East, and Africa. However, he wanted to go even farther than Marco Polo had. In the 14th century, he set out on a journey that would last nearly 30 years, visiting lands across North Africa, the Middle East, India, China, and Southeast Asia.

Ibn Battuta confirmed many of the things that Marco Polo had written about the Mongol Empire, particularly about China's wealth, organization, and large cities. While some European readers had doubted Marco's stories, Ibn Battuta's accounts provided further evidence that these lands were as vast and advanced as Marco had described. His travels added even more details to what the world knew about Asia and expanded the understanding of global trade and culture.

The Portuguese explorer **Vasco da Gama** was also influenced by the desire to find direct routes to the lands Marco Polo had written about. In the late 1400s, Portugal was looking for ways to bypass overland trade routes and reach the wealth of the East by sea. Using information gathered from earlier travelers, Vasco da Gama sailed around the southern tip of Africa, successfully reaching India in 1498. His journey proved that direct sea trade with Asia was possible, opening a new chapter in world exploration.

Another well-known figure who admired Marco Polo's work was **Ferdinand Magellan**, the explorer who led the first expedition to sail around the world. Magellan and his crew were driven by the same goals that had guided Marco Polo and other travelers before him—the search for wealth, knowledge, and new trade routes. His expedition confirmed that the world was far larger than most Europeans had previously thought, an idea that Marco's book had first helped introduce.

The Age of Exploration Begins

Marco Polo's journey ended when he returned to Venice, but his stories lived on. His book introduced Europeans to lands they had never seen, describing cities larger than any in Europe, rulers more powerful than their own kings, and trade routes that connected the world in ways most people had never imagined. While some doubted his claims, others saw them as an invitation—a challenge to explore the unknown. Over the next few centuries, his stories helped spark a period of discovery that would come to be known as the Age of Exploration.

Before Marco Polo's time, European maps were small and incomplete. Most people had little understanding of the world beyond the Mediterranean. They knew about parts of the Middle East and North Africa, but beyond that, much of the world was a mystery. His book provided one of the first detailed descriptions of lands stretching across Asia, giving mapmakers new information to work with.

As his stories spread, European rulers and

merchants became more interested in finding better ways to reach the lands he had described. The Silk Road had long been the main route connecting Europe to Asia, but it was slow and expensive. Traders had to cross mountains, deserts, and dangerous territories, and each stop along the way meant paying fees to different rulers. The idea of finding a faster route, one that could bring silk and spices directly to Europe, became more appealing.

This search for new trade routes would eventually lead to some of the greatest voyages in history. Portuguese explorers, eager to reach Asia by sea, began sailing farther down the coast of Africa. In 1498, Vasco da Gama became the first European to sail directly to India, opening up a new path for trade. His journey proved that the wealth of the East could be reached without crossing the overland routes controlled by Middle Eastern traders.

At the same time, Spain was looking for its own way to the riches of Asia. Christopher Columbus, inspired by Marco Polo's descriptions, believed he could reach the East by sailing west across the Atlantic Ocean. Though he miscalculated the distance and instead landed in the Americas, his voyage changed history. His discoveries led to further exploration of the New World, connecting

Europe to lands that had previously been unknown to them.

Explorers like Ferdinand Magellan and later European navigators continued pushing the boundaries of what was known, mapping new territories and proving that the world was much larger than many had believed. While they did not follow Marco Polo's exact path, the ideas in his book had helped set their journeys in motion.

The Age of Exploration was not just about finding new lands—it was about expanding knowledge. European scientists, geographers, and merchants studied the reports of travelers, comparing them to Marco Polo's accounts. They updated maps, tested new navigation techniques, and learned from the cultures they encountered. The exchange of ideas, goods, and knowledge between continents reshaped the world in ways that still affect global trade and exploration today.

CONCLUSION: WHAT WE CAN LEARN FROM MARCO POLO

Marco Polo's travels may have taken place centuries ago, but the lessons from his journey are still important today. His story is not just about trade routes, powerful emperors, or distant lands—it is about curiosity, determination, and the willingness to step into the unknown. He was not a conqueror, a king, or a soldier. He was a merchant, an explorer, and a storyteller, and through his observations, the world learned more about places that had been largely unknown to Europeans.

One of the most important lessons from Marco Polo's life is the value of curiosity. He was raised in Venice, a city full of merchants and traders, but he did not just want to sell goods—he wanted to understand the world beyond what he had been taught.

While many people in his time were content to stay in familiar places, Marco was eager to learn about different cultures, governments, and inventions. His ability to ask questions and observe new customs made him stand out. He did not assume that the way things were done in Europe was the only way or the best way. Instead, he paid attention to the advanced cities, technologies, and trade systems of the Mongol Empire, realizing that Europe could learn from them.

Another lesson from Marco Polo's journey is the importance of resilience. Traveling in the 13th century was not easy. There were no airplanes, no modern maps, and no guarantees of safety along the way. He faced deserts, mountains, and oceans, often traveling for months without knowing exactly what lay ahead. Even when he and his family wanted to return home, they had to wait for the right opportunity, knowing that leaving too soon might be dangerous. Instead of giving up when the journey was difficult, Marco adapted to new environments, learning new languages and customs to survive.

His travels also show the power of communication. Marco Polo did more than just travel—he listened, learned, and later shared what he had seen. Without his book, most Europeans would have remained unaware of the vast world beyond their borders. His ability to describe cities, inventions, and cultures allowed others to see what he had experienced, even if they never left their own country. His book connected people in a time when there were no telephones, newspapers, or the internet.

Trade and cultural exchange were also central themes in Marco's journey. While he traveled for business, his experiences went beyond selling goods. He witnessed how different regions traded not just silk and spices, but also ideas. He saw Buddhist temples alongside Muslim mosques, met Persian scholars working in China, and encountered inventions that had been passed from one civilization to another. His travels showed that the world was already connected in many ways, even before ships crossed the Atlantic or explorers mapped the globe.

Another key lesson is the idea that exploration does not always mean conquering. Many historical figures who traveled to new lands did so with armies, seeking to take control through force. Marco Polo traveled with curiosity rather than weapons. He was welcomed into Kublai Khan's court not because he was a warrior, but because he was willing to learn and observe. His journey reminds us that exploration does not have to be about claiming land or defeating enemies—it can also be about understanding and sharing knowledge.

Doubt and skepticism also played a role in his legacy. Many people refused to believe his stories, thinking they were too incredible to be real. Even though his book described real places and customs, some readers dismissed it as fiction. Yet, centuries later, many of his accounts were confirmed. His experience teaches that new ideas can often be met with doubt, but that does not mean they are untrue. Pioneers and explorers throughout history have faced disbelief, only to be proven right over time.

The Spirit of Adventure Today

Marco Polo lived in a time when the world felt much bigger and more mysterious than it does today. There were no airplanes, no internet, no satellite maps showing every corner of the planet. The idea of traveling across continents was dangerous, unpredictable, and filled with uncertainty. Yet, he embraced that challenge. He set out on a journey that changed not only his life but the way people understood the world.

That same spirit of adventure still exists today, even though the world looks very different. The days of traveling on horseback through unknown lands may be over, but there are still discoveries to be made. New technologies, scientific breakthroughs, and unexplored regions of the deep ocean and outer space offer modern adventurers a chance to push the boundaries of what is known. While the kinds of journeys people take may have changed, the mindset of an explorer—the desire to learn, experience, and understand—remains just as important.

Curiosity is one of the biggest lessons from Marco Polo's travels. He didn't just pass through different cities and countries—he asked questions, paid attention, and wanted to learn how things worked. Whether it was the way people governed their lands, how they built their cities, or what they ate and wore, he took the time to observe and understand. That same curiosity is valuable today. Asking questions about the world, wanting to learn about different cultures, and staying open to new ideas are all ways people can still embrace the spirit of adventure.

Travel itself is much easier now than it was in Marco Polo's time. A journey that once took years can now be made in hours by plane. But even though getting from one place to another is simpler, the opportunity to explore and experience new things is still there. Visiting new countries, meeting people with different traditions, and learning new languages are ways to continue what Marco Polo started centuries ago. His journey was not just about reaching faraway lands—it was about understanding them.

The idea of adventure is not limited to travel. Scientific discoveries, medical advancements, and space exploration all require the same kind of courage and curiosity that Marco Polo had. Scientists exploring the ocean depths, astronauts studying other planets, and engineers developing new technology all share the same mindset—seeking the unknown and learning from what they find. The spirit of adventure is not just about going to new places, but about looking at the world with curiosity and a desire to learn.

Another lesson from Marco Polo's journey is that stepping outside of what is familiar can lead to great discoveries. He could have stayed in Venice and continued his family's business, but he chose to go beyond what was expected. That decision led him to experiences most people in his time could not have imagined. Taking risks, trying new things, and pushing beyond what feels comfortable can lead to unexpected and exciting opportunities.

Communication and storytelling also play a big role in adventure. If Marco Polo had traveled to China but never written about it, his experiences would have been lost to history. Sharing knowledge —whether through books, conversations, or technology—is how ideas spread. Today, people can learn about other cultures, history, and science through videos, articles, and books. The spirit of adventure is not just about experiencing new things but about sharing them with others.

Even though much of the world has been mapped and explored, there are always new things to discover. Whether it's learning about a different culture, asking questions about how something works, or seeking out new knowledge, the lessons from Marco Polo's journey still apply today. He showed that the world is bigger than what most people see every day and that those who are willing to explore—whether across lands or through ideas —can change how others see the world.

Exploring the World in Modern Times

Exploration today is not always about discovering new lands, but about learning more about the world and the people in it. Marco Polo was not just a traveler; he was an observer. He paid attention to the details of life in the Mongol Empire—how people lived, what they ate, how they governed themselves, and how they traded. That same kind of curiosity is just as important today. While the world has been mapped, there are still countless cultures, traditions, and ways of life that people can learn about.

One of the biggest differences between Marco Polo's time and today is how people can share their discoveries. In the 13th century, information spread slowly. Books had to be copied by hand, and few people could read. Today, stories, pictures, and experiences can be shared instantly. A person traveling in another country can document their journey through videos, blogs, or social media, allowing people on the other side of the world to learn from them in real-time. The ability to communicate quickly means that ideas, cultures, and innovations can be exchanged faster than ever.

Technology has also changed how people explore. Satellites provide images of distant planets, deep-sea submarines allow scientists to study the ocean floor, and artificial intelligence helps researchers analyze data in ways that were impossible in Marco Polo's time. While he traveled by horse, ship, and foot, modern explorers use spacecraft, submarines, and digital tools to continue expanding what is known about the universe.

Even though travel is easier, it still requires an open mind. Marco Polo's journey was not just about reaching new places—it was about understanding them. He learned different languages, observed customs, and respected traditions that were different from his own. Today, people have the same opportunity to learn from others. Whether through travel, books, or conversations, exploring different perspectives is one of the most valuable ways to grow.

Trade was a major part of Marco Polo's journey, and global trade remains important today. The clothes people wear, the food they eat, and the technology they use often come from different parts of the world. Understanding how countries are connected through trade, economy, and culture is a way to continue exploring, even without leaving home.

Exploration also happens in science and innovation. Medical researchers develop new treatments, engineers design new forms of transportation, and scientists look for life on other planets. Each of these efforts requires curiosity, persistence, and a willingness to push beyond what is already known. Just as Marco Polo described paper money and bridges that seemed impossible to Europeans at the time, modern explorers continue to introduce new discoveries that reshape how people think about the world.

There are still parts of the Earth that remain largely unexplored. The deep ocean, for example, holds mysteries about marine life and ecosystems that scientists are only beginning to understand. Space exploration continues to push boundaries, with missions to Mars and beyond aiming to uncover more about the universe. While the physical map of the world may be complete, the search for knowledge is far from over.

The lessons from Marco Polo's journey are still relevant. Being curious, open to learning, and willing to step outside of what is familiar are qualities that continue to shape exploration. His journey may have taken place centuries ago, but the spirit of discovery remains just as important today.

APPENDIX

Words We Use Today Because of Marco Polo

1. "Silk"

Silk existed in Europe before Marco Polo's journey, but it was rare and extremely valuable. His book helped increase interest in silk, making it one of the most sought-after trade goods. He described how the Chinese produced silk from silkworms and how their weaving techniques were more advanced than anything in Europe. Over time, as more silk was imported, the word became widely used. Today, silk is a common material, but during Marco Polo's time, it was considered a luxury only the wealthiest people could afford.

2. "Ginger"

Marco Polo was one of the first Europeans to describe how ginger was used in Asian cooking and medicine. At the time, spices were incredibly valuable, and traders made huge profits bringing them to Europe. Marco Polo's descriptions of ginger encouraged merchants to bring more of it to the West, and the word became widely known. Today, ginger is used in teas, cookies, and many types of food, but in Marco Polo's time, it was considered an exotic spice.

3. "Pasta"

Many people believe Marco Polo brought pasta to Italy from China, but the truth is a little different. Italians already had a form of pasta before his journey. However, Marco Polo wrote about **noodles** in China and how they were a staple food there. Some historians think his descriptions helped make pasta more popular in Europe. While the word "pasta" itself may not have come from Marco Polo, his writings helped spread knowledge about different ways of making and eating noodles.

4. "Porcelain"

One of the items Marco Polo described in detail was **porcelain**, a type of fine ceramic pottery that was much stronger and smoother than anything made in Europe at the time. Chinese artisans had mastered the art of making porcelain centuries before Europeans even knew about it. Marco Polo's book introduced the word and the idea of this beautiful, delicate material to the West. Today, porcelain is used in dishes, decorations, and even bathroom fixtures, but in the 13th century, it was considered an incredible luxury.

5. "Khan"

The word **Khan**, meaning ruler or leader, came from the Mongol Empire. Marco Polo frequently referred to Kublai Khan, the emperor of China, using this title. While Europeans were familiar with kings and emperors, the term "Khan" was new to them. Over time, the word entered various languages, often being used to describe powerful leaders or even as a last name in some cultures.

6. "Yurt"

Marco Polo described the homes of Mongol nomads, which were round, portable tents made of wood and felt. These were called **yurts**, and they allowed Mongol warriors to move quickly across vast territories without needing to build permanent houses. The word stuck, and today, people still use yurts for camping and living spaces in some parts of the world.

7. "Paper Money"

While Marco Polo didn't invent paper money, he

was one of the first Europeans to write about it. In China, Kublai Khan's empire used paper currency instead of gold and silver coins. At the time, this idea seemed impossible to Europeans, who thought only metal coins had real value. Marco Polo's descriptions of paper money eventually helped introduce the concept to Europe, where it slowly became more accepted. Today, almost every country in the world uses paper money or digital currency instead of relying only on gold and silver.

8. "Sequin"

The word **sequin**, which refers to a small, shiny coin-shaped decoration often used on clothing, originally came from a type of coin that Marco Polo encountered. The **zecchino** was a gold coin used in Venice, and the name eventually evolved into the word "sequin." Over time, the meaning shifted from money to small metallic decorations, but its origin is connected to trade and travel during Marco Polo's era.

9. "Galleon"

Ships were a big part of Marco Polo's journey, and his descriptions of large sailing vessels helped introduce new ship designs to Europeans. The word **galleon**, which describes a large, multi-decked sailing ship, is believed to have been influenced by the types of ships Marco Polo encountered. These ships became important for trade and exploration in later centuries.

Try This! A Silk Road Trade Game

How to Play the Silk Road Trade Game

This game is designed to be played with friends, family, or classmates. Each player takes on the role of a trader traveling along the Silk Road, starting with a set amount of goods and coins. The goal is to travel to different cities, trade wisely, and return home with the most valuable collection of goods.

Materials Needed:

- Small slips of paper to represent different goods (e.g., silk, spices, gold, jade, horses, glass, paper, tea).
- Coins or tokens to represent money.
- A game board or a simple drawn map of the Silk Road with key trading cities (e.g., Venice, Baghdad, Samarkand, Kashgar, Beijing).
- A six-sided die (or a spinner) to determine travel success.

- Event cards with different challenges (e.g., "Bandits stole some of your goods! Lose one item." or "You find a wealthy buyer! Double your profit on one trade.").

Setting Up the Game

Each player starts in **Venice**, one of the major trading cities of Europe. They receive five coins and three random trade goods. The goal is to make it to **Beijing**, China, buy and sell goods along the way, and return home with the most wealth.

Each turn, players move to a new city by rolling the die. The number rolled determines how many spaces they move. Some cities have specific items that are cheaper to buy, while others pay more for certain goods.

Trading Rules

1. Each city has a market where certain goods are in high demand, meaning they sell for more coins. Other goods might be common there, making them cheaper to buy.
2. Players can buy and sell goods in each city they stop at, trying to earn a profit.

3. If a player does not have enough coins to buy new goods, they must barter with another player or wait for an opportunity to trade.

Challenges Along the Way

Traveling on the Silk Road was not always easy. Each time a player moves, they must draw an **event card** that could affect their journey. These cards might help or hurt them. Here are some examples:

- **"Sandstorm! Lose a turn while you wait for the storm to pass."**
- **"A wealthy merchant in Samarkand is looking for high-quality silk. If you have silk, you can sell it for double the price."**
- **"Your caravan is attacked by bandits! Lose one random trade good."**
- **"A friendly local helps you find the best deals. You may buy one extra good this turn at half price."**

Players must adapt to these challenges, just like real merchants on the Silk Road.

Winning the Game

Once players make it to Beijing, they can choose to turn around and head back to Venice or continue trading in nearby cities. The game ends when all players have returned home. The player with the most valuable goods and coins at the end wins.

Fun Facts About Silk Road Trade

- The Silk Road got its name because silk was one of the most valuable goods traded, but many other items were exchanged, including spices, tea, glass, and even ideas like mathematics and medicine.
- Travelers used **camels** to carry heavy loads through deserts because they could survive long periods without water.
- Many different languages were spoken along the Silk Road, so merchants had to find ways to communicate, often using hand gestures or hiring translators.
- Some merchants never traveled the entire route. Instead, they sold goods at one city, and another merchant would take them farther.

Activity: Create Your Own Trade Route

Using a blank world map, mark a trade route from your home to a distant location. What items would you trade along the way? How would different regions affect the prices of goods? What challenges might you face?

www.ingramcontent.com/pod-product-compliance
Ingram Content Group UK Ltd.
Pitfield, Milton Keynes, MK11 3LW, UK
UKHW020839150225
455111UK00012B/646